The Interpreter's Guide to Life:

365 TIPS

for Interpreters

*('Don't wear black to a wedding'
and other words of advice)*

Jack Hoza, Ph.D.

ISBN 1-881133-19-2

How to order

Copies may be ordered from Sign Media, Inc., 4020
Blackburn Lane, Burtonsville, MD 20866-1167. For credit
card orders, place your order online at *www.signmedia.com*
or phone 1-800-475-4756.

Foreword

Jack Hoza's book is a collection of clear, readable ideas important to interpreters. On the surface it may appear to be a handbook of "tips" providing advice on issues common to people in the interpreting field.

In fact, this book covers a wide range of aspects of our work, the field, and us. Some of the subjects are practical and concrete such as pointers on business and financial matters which are useful for those of us who are self-employed.

Several interwoven themes presented in this book invite the reader to think more deeply about matters that are not always discussed in training materials. Many of the concepts relate to our ethical positions, elevating the profession, preparing for assignments, and decision-making. Others directly address ways to deal with challenges that occur during the task of interpreting. Jack Hoza also includes comments on the broader philosophical perspectives that influence our work.

In my many years of teaching interpreting, I have come to appreciate the importance of working with the psychological and emotional demands of this work. This book includes important advice on taking care of ourselves and nurturing our growth. Take these seriously. They are guides for life.

You can use this book in many ways. Read a page each day and spend some time reflecting on your thoughts and feelings; go through the book and identify areas that you feel are most illuminating or challenging to you and which may form the basis for setting goals for yourself; and share these ideas with colleagues, consumers, friends, and family.

Betty M. Colonomos,
College Park, MD

Introduction

We have all experienced times when it has been difficult to express our own thoughts, yet it is an interpreter's goal to consistently relay other people's thoughts clearly and accurately. Add to this the fact that interpreters work in a variety of settings and work with people from all walks of life, and it is easy to see why the life of an interpreter is both intriguing and challenging. Indeed, the life of an interpreter involves managing the interpreting process and making quick decisions to successfully deal with the following: a wide range of language users, a myriad of multi-cultural perspectives and expectations, varied topics and discourse genres, challenges to personal and professional integrity, and changing interpersonal dynamics. Interpreters make decisions regarding all of these factors while trying to maintain a good, working relationship with the participants, and striving to main-tain a role that fosters trust, works for the setting, and reflects well on this bicultural/multicultural profession.

Interpretation is a complex task that varies with each situation. Because of the need to constantly explore these various factors, the learning process of interpreters never ends; it is, by necessity, life-long.

This book attempts to address the multitude of issues faced by bilingual/multilingual individuals functioning as interpreters, and is the result of observations that I have made during my many years as an interpreter and interpreter educator. The pointers in this book come not only from my own observations and thoughts, but also from innumerable conversations with hundreds of interpreters, interpreting students, Deaf people, and hearing people with whom it has been my pleasure to work and to be acquainted over the years. The tips are a compilation of lessons learned and an attempt to capture some of the intuitions and 'tips of the trade' of more experienced and trusted interpreters. I hope that interpreting students, newer interpreters, seasoned interpreters, those who work with interpreters, and others interested in interpretation will benefit from these tips.

Many of the tips included in this book do not appear in interpreter education curricula, but rather are learned from experience in the profession, from conversations with colleagues, and by interacting with the communities which interpreters serve. This book seeks to clarify some of the implications and obligations that arise in interpreting. Some of the tips are common sense, while others are common sense to those who have 'been there and done that', and yet others require more thought and self-reflection. But all of these tips should provide the reader with food for thought on how to live the life of an interpreter, what it is that interpreters are trying to do, and what the implications are of our decisions as interpreters.

In short, this book attempts to provide practical tips, helpful strategies, and words of advice to help newer interpreters get off on the right foot, to provide more seasoned interpreters with issues to think about, and to help the people we work with gain a better sense of the life of the interpreter.

Jack Hoza
June 5, 2003
Newburyport, MA

DEDICATION

To my Deaf parents, Dorothy and
the late Raymond Hoza,
and to interpreters of good
conscience everywhere

1.

Don't overbook. It inevitably
leads to unhappy consumers and
a stressed out interpreter.

2.

If you deviate from the
Code of Ethics, always be prepared
to explain why you did so.

3.

Know what is and is not
a business expense.

4.

Be a consumer of interpreting services at least once a year; it's good to be in the consumer's shoes.

5.

Be considerate of interpreter
referral specialists;
they have a tough job.

6.

Aristotle had it right:
"An unexamined life is not
worth living." An interpreter
who leads an unexamined life
may not be worth hiring.

7.

If you are in private practice,
work with a financial planner
to plan for your retirement.

8.

If you are concerned

that something will come

back to haunt you,

it probably will.

9.

Take seriously the tenet
to use discretion in accepting
assignments; people deserve
what they pay for.

10.

Interpreters strive not to engage
in the content of an interaction,
so balance your work with
activities in which you can be
an active participant.

11.

Develop skills to remain centered
during your work.

12.

Consumers have their own idea of what the role of an interpreter is. Be sure that you communicate clearly what you see as part of your role and what you do not.

13.

When interpreting on the telephone,
describe what the Deaf person is
doing if she is not signing, e.g.,
"Just a moment. Let me get a pen."
It could keep the other person
from hanging up.

14.

Flexibility keeps us sane and
consumers happy.

15.

Learn all you can about
overuse syndrome and make sure
you don't become a victim.

16.

Never take a job that

Deaf people consider

a 'Deaf job'.

17.

Consider how these two terms differ:
professionalism and *profession*.
The first has to do with our individual
behavior and the second is the
culmination of all of us. What is your
contribution to the profession?

18.

Maintain a balance between
work and play.

19.

Keep your sense of humor.

20.

Remember that whatever

you do, you are setting

a precedent for

the next interpreter.

21.

Ethics has to do with right and wrong,
so follow your intuition as well
as your ethical training. Remember
your sense of fairness.

22.

If you can't sleep at night because of
an interpreting assignment, talk
confidentially to another interpreter
about what is eating you.

23.

Have a way of dealing with
overwhelming feelings.

24.

Our professional ethics need

to be sensitive to the cross-

cultural contexts in which

we find ourselves. Our ethics

should be neither strictly

'hearing' nor 'Deaf', but rather

a carefully considered

combination of the two.

25.

Attend to the general impressions
that participants are trying to
give each other and the general
impressions that come across
in your interpretation.

26.

Dress to respect everyone in the setting
and not to embarrass anyone.

27.

Be aware of your own biases.
We owe it to the people we work with
to keep an eye on our filters.

28.

Stand up for yourself;

do not give into unreasonable

requests. Interpreters like

to think they are 'invisible',

but to disempower ourselves

is to disempower those for

whom we interpret.

29.

Practice clear communication.
Asking, "*Who* was it that went
to Chicago?" is clearer than
"What did you say?"

30.

We do not interpret 'languages',
we interpret for people who are
using language at a particular time
for a particular purpose.

31.

Work on advancing your
education; this is how a profession
is recognized.

32.

Mentor a beginning interpreter;

you both benefit.

33.

Keep breath mints on hand.

34.

Keep in mind the distinction
between 'good help', which allows
people to accomplish their own goals,
and 'bad help', which attempts to
get people to accomplish *our* goals.

35.

Being hearing is not a
'four-letter word';
mis-using power is.

36.

Have short one-line

responses ready for commonly

asked questions.

37.

We are not 'telephones'.
We use our intuition about people,
language usage, settings,
interaction, and culture to convey
comparable meaning. I've never
seen a telephone do that!

38.

There is no such thing as a
'generalist'; we all specialize
in certain areas. Be aware of
your areas of expertise.

39.

Don't wear black to a wedding.

40.

After each interpreting assignment, reflect on what you have learned about ethics, interaction, the interpreting process, or working as a part of an interpreting team.

41.

Have a nice jacket (or tie)
in the car in case you need to
dress up unexpectedly.

42.

Don't participate in a meeting and
interpret the same meeting.
It's not fair to you or to consumers.

43.

If you are self-employed,
a good CPA is worth the money.

44.

Attend to how native

ASL signers and English

speakers express themselves

in various natural settings;

they are our language models.

45.

If you use a bilingual-bicultural
model, be aware that it includes
various language varieties
and cultural variation; don't
assume only two languages and
two cultures are at play.

46.

Expect naive questions from
consumers; patience will pay off.

47.

Watch your boundaries;
healthy boundaries lead to
healthy interpreters.

48.

Encourage the use of

Deaf interpreters.

49.

Study geography and current events;
they will come in handy.

50.

If you are positioned so that the
Deaf consumer cannot see you
and the hearing consumer at the
same time, avoid the ping-pong effect,
and move. Don't have the
Deaf consumer suffer it out.

51.

Let consumers know that you take
confidentiality seriously.

52.

Don't speak for the

Deaf community.

53.

Talk to spoken language
interpreters about their work;
we have a lot to learn
from each other.

54.

Don't interpret the funeral of
someone you knew well;
you need to grieve.

55.

Learn to make decisions quickly.
Remember that not to
decide is a decision.

56.

Support multiculturalism in the interpreting field.

57.

Anticipate potential cross-cultural conflicts and have strategies for dealing with them.

58.

Be considerate. Be sure to turn off electronic devices (pagers, cell phones) during assignments, or put them on vibrate mode.

59.

Join and be an active member of interpreter organizations—both local and national.

60.

Be respectful at all times.

You are a guest in other

people's lives.

61.

Always consider cultural nuances and differences when determining an equivalent in the Target Language. It could make or break the interpretation; interpreting is not only about language.

62.

Compare yourself to yourself, not to others.

63.

Knowing languages is not enough; we must know *about* languages.

64.

Research the latest

information on topics you

interpret; having prior

knowledge is half the job.

65.

Be aware of the Deaf grapevine.
What you are doing as an interpreter
will become common knowledge.
Think of this as a consumer system
of checks and balances.

66.

Professional behavior means being
confident and acting like you
know something—without making
others feel like they don't.

67.

Be aware of your own stressors and
have ways to alleviate stress in your life.

68.

We all need mentors.

Find one who truly listens

to you and is able to help

you think clearly about

your own progress.

69.

Provide support to other interpreters,
but avoid empty comments like,
"You did a good job." Focus on specifics
and stick to what you can objectively
state, i.e., what you can hear or see.
You don't know what was going
on in their mind at the time.

70.

Listen to Deaf people's stories and
remember the moral of these stories.

71.

Speak up when unqualified people are
hired to interpret; it is unjust.

72.

Remember the Code of Ethics is not a shield to protect you from ethical decision-making, but rather a guide to ensure ethical fairness and to protect consumers and yourself.

73.

A talented interpreter knows how to
get others to buy into her ideas.
Clear explanations, an open attitude,
and a clear desire to make things work
are all key to effective negotiation.

74.

Keep discussions of billing and
payment for the party you bill;
don't discuss these with consumers.

75.

Learn from seasoned interpreters
who have the most recent
training and education.

76.

Don't interpret until
you understand.
People can wait, and everyone
will be glad they did.

77.

Don't interpret 'whispering' in ASL;
just because you can see it doesn't
mean it was intended to be interpreted.
If you are unsure if something
should be interpreted, ask.

78.

Be early to an assignment;
being prompt isn't enough and
being late can be a disaster.

79.

Be familiar with federal and
state interpreter laws.

80.

Remember we always

represent the 'other culture'

to consumers.

81.

Watch for 'false friends', i.e., words
and signs that at first glance seem to
match in meaning, but don't.
Wait a second to come up with a more
semantic equivalent.

82.

During 'down time' (when you're not
interpreting), don't just talk shop.

83.

Establish a routine for physically
warming up before interpreting and
cooling down afterwards.

84.

Practice consecutive

interpreting; it will

enhance your simultaneous

interpreting work.

85.

Have blank invoices on hand.

86.

Never interpret when your
hands are cold.

87.

Be aware that an interpreting situation
can become a 'legal' interpreting
assignment at any moment.
Know when to call in a
specialized legal interpreter.

88.

Know what comprises the downside of the job and deal with these things to avoid burn-out.

89.

Have good, detailed maps of
the cities and region in
which you work.

90.

Learn regional—as well as
nationally recognized—signs
and acronyms.

91.

When interpreting a play
into ASL, work with a Deaf ASL
consultant.

92.

Expect anything. You may
be surprised by something
during an interpreting
assignment, but don't let it
show; remain professional.

93.

Before a meeting begins,
make a seating chart of people's
names and/or name signs.

94.

Interpret all the information a
Deaf person needs to know *before*
he goes under anesthesia or
has his eyes dilated.

95.

When interpreting for terminal
patients, be sure to get additional
support for yourself.

96.

Strive to understand how you manage the interpreting process: dropping form, representing meaning, composing meaning, and making decisions about cultural mediation, language equivalency, discourse structure, etc. These are at the heart of interpreting and are what separate interpreters from other bilinguals/multilinguals.

97.

Work on your self-esteem so
it doesn't adversely affect your
interpreting work.

98.

Avoid hobbies that involve fine
motor movements, such as knitting
or playing computer games.

99.

Use a pager; they are a godsend
especially when there are cancellations.

100.

Develop a strong sense of
what it is like to understand
without words; this sense
is the crux of interpretation.

101.

Friends and family may not understand
what you do, but they know *you*,
and that is even more important;
don't forget friends and family.

102.

Find a simple way to keep good tax
records that works for you.

103.

Separate the interpretation from
the interpreter—and include
your own work in this.

104.

Be aware of how the other

gender uses language and

explore how you can best

match such language use.

105.

Don't underestimate the value of a
good, well-rounded education.

106.

Talk to Deaf consumers about
your background (how you
got into the field, Deaf people you
know, and the events in your life).
This connection is important.

107.

Always ask for clarification—
unless it is totally inappropriate to
do so, as with a formal lecture.

108.

The interpreting model interpreters work under defines them; find a model that best provides a framework for your interpreting work and ethical decisions.

109.

Interpreters often know a little
about a lot; break the mold,
learn a lot about a lot.

110.

If it seems that you may be needed
beyond the scheduled time of an
assignment, let the people involved
know immediately how long
you can realistically stay.

111.

When interpreting outdoors,
don't wear sunglasses.

112.

If you don't have a Deaf mentor, you are missing out.

113.

When interpreting for children,
remember how *big* you are in
the eyes of a child.

114.

Work on increasing your vocabulary
in ASL and English by either setting
up a systematic approach to
studying vocabulary or by finding out
the meanings of new words/signs
as you encounter them.

115.

When in doubt,
dress up a bit more.

116.

Develop both kinds of credentials that we have in our field:

1) paper credentials, such as degrees and certifications, and

2) community credentials, which involve consumers recommending you due to your 'attitude' and your ability to be conscientious and to work well with people.

117.

Know the names of state and national leaders (both Deaf and hearing); their names will undoubtedly come up.

118.

If you feel you are getting in a rut, do something that will change your frame of reference. Expand your mind by attending a workshop or talking to people who inspire you.

119.

Don't flirt with consumers.

120.

Learning from one person is

never enough. Be sure to

expose yourself to a variety

of interpreters and Deaf people.

The differences in viewpoints

can be illuminating.

121.

Develop an understanding of—and comfort level with—the notions of *collectivistic culture* and *individualistic culture*, and how they relate to the realities of your work. Interpreters work with both types of cultures.

122.

If you're having difficulty with someone, first respectfully acknowledge this person's perspective and feelings, then work from there.

123.

Don't overuse the 'WHY?' rhetorical question in ASL.

124.

Interpreting is not a nine

to five job; it is a career

with a particular community.

It is a life choice.

Respect this choice.

125.

Remember that the people you work with are depending on you to know when they can enter a conversation. Be aware of the signals you are giving regarding turn-taking during an interaction.

126.

Physically relax when you can. Take up yoga, go to a massage therapist, or just go on a walk.

127.

Be sure the Deaf person knows that translation is an option when written English is involved.

128.

Watch your body language and where you position yourself in an interpreting assignment. These non-verbal cues will likely be interpreted by consumers as your allegiance to certain parties in the interaction.

129.

Not all people get along.
Keep your sanity and make sure you
avoid unnecessary squabbling.
Maintain your support system.

130.

Be wary of people who bunch all
problems into one category.
Power, culture, or ethics alone cannot
account for everything.

131.

We are our own worst critics.
Pat yourself on the back as well as focus
on what you would like to do better.

132.

Activities affecting the

Deaf community require

Deaf community involvement.

Work to make this happen

in the interpreting field.

133.

If you have heard some juicy gossip, don't spread it. However, if you know some good news (and it was not derived from an interpreting assignment), share that. We have a unique place in the Deaf community grapevine. Tread carefully.

134.

Don't make up signs; it is an insult to ASL and the Deaf community. Always consult with a Deaf person savvy on the topic about how to sign something.

135.

Be the type of interpreter that you would trust to interpret for your loved ones.

136.

If you really are not happy

as an interpreter, it is better

to switch professions before

your feelings begin to

affect your work and the people

for whom you interpret.

137.

A narrative, a description,
an interview, a lecture, a joke, and
a conversation are all quite different.
Study how these discourse genres
are structured in ASL and English,
and attend to these differences in
your interpreting.

138.

Be aware of how you are affecting
the interaction. Is the focus on the
participants' interaction?

139.

Wear comfortable, but
appropriate, shoes.

140.

If you have a unique skill or

idea, be sure to share it with

the field in some way.

Write an article, present a

workshop, or talk to students

in an interpreting program.

This is one way reciprocity works

in the interpreting field.

141.

Sometimes interpreters chalk up differences between Deaf and hearing people to the difference in their hearing status. Look at these differences as cultural or linguistic differences, and you are more likely to understand them.

142.

In most settings, greet the Deaf people first.

143.

If you are using a lot of prepositions in your ASL rendition, you are probably not really signing ASL.

144.

If a Deaf person says that
something you are wearing or
something you are doing is
visually distracting, believe her,
and remedy the distraction.

145.

Attend to what makes you feel
in control of the interpreting process,
and focus on how you can make this
happen consistently.

146.

Never say, "I'm just the interpreter."
You're not 'just' anything.
Better to say your point clearly,
e.g., do you mean that as the interpreter
you do not participate in the discussion?
Say what you really mean.

147.

Learn how to project your voice
(for when the speaker system is down).

148.

Remember that explaining your

role once is never enough.

Expect the need to clarify your

role with consumers at times.

149.

Challenge your skills at times by
taking assignments that are a bit
more difficult than you are comfortable
with. Stretch your comfort zone;
you'll learn some things.

150.

Be mindful of when a speaker is being
implicit and the audience immediately
gets what goes 'unsaid'. You may need to
make certain information *explicit* to
convey equivalent meaning.

151.

Be aware of classism, and be careful
not to contribute to it.

152.

Remember we do not
interpret for Deaf people;
we interpret for Deaf *and*
hearing people.

153.

The trick to interpreting conversations, discussions, and telephone calls is interpreting quickly, yet clearly, because these interactions are so fast-paced. Figure out strategies for doing these types of assignments as successfully as possible.

154.

Record your interpretation sometimes to review and learn from your own work.

155.

Read any good books or articles lately? Share them with others.

156.

If you want people to cooperate with you, start by cooperating with them.

157.

If you interpret lectures but have never given one, you need to experience giving a lecture. If you're not sure where to begin, check out workshops, classes, or the local Toastmasters' chapter in your area.

158.

When do you hug and when do you not hug? If you are not certain, let the other person initiate a hug.

159.

When interpreting with several Deaf people, maintain eye contact equally among them; don't favor just one or two.

160.

We do not help people succeed.

We provide a service

that may allow them to

succeed—or fail.

161.

Remember it takes special expertise to interpret for the mentally ill. Do not make talk that is nonsensical sound sensible in the interpretation. The mental health professional needs to assess this person's thinking processes.

162.

We need to feel a little pressure to keep us on task, but too much can paralyze us. Be aware of the level of pressure you feel and if it is helping you or hindering you.

163.

If you have a beard or mustache, keep it trimmed.

164.

Have a good list of back-up
interpreters in case you
need to call on them to
substitute for you.

165.

Interpreters don't often have an opportunity to see a wide range of registers in their second language. Be sure to interact socially and professionally with a wide range of Deaf people, and to attend—or watch videotapes of— formal presentations in ASL.

166.

If asked by the Deaf community to serve on a committee, say, "Yes," if at all possible.

167.

Saying "Please" and "Thank you" can work wonders with English speakers.

168.

Listen to interpreters who think like you do, but also listen to those who don't.

169.

If you have interpreted a question and the answer seems off base, stop the situation and state that the interpreter needs a moment to clarify. Interpreters have an obligation not to make people look stupid if the interpretation was not clear.

170.

Some people are 'feeling people' and some people are 'thinking people'. Know which you are and recognize that others may approach the world in a different way.

171.

Volunteer to be on at least one committee.

172.

Be sure to clearly differentiate between interpreting and transliterating in your work; strive not to intermingle the two.

173.

If you have interpreted a traumatic experience or have witnessed extreme oppression, be sure to get the mental health support you need.

174.

Have information with you on interpreter referral agencies and other agencies that serve the Deaf community in your area— in case people need that information.

175.

Some people are easy to get along with and some aren't. Learn how to cope with all kinds of people and don't think you have to like everyone.

176.

Pick a team member you can

work well with, but at times

work with others and

try to increase your ability

to work as a team with

a variety of interpreters.

177.

If a person is using simultaneous communication (sim-com) and some people are not able to follow what he is saying, offer the choice of his using either English or ASL— and let him know that you can interpret into the other language for him.

178.

Make sure your immunizations are up-to-date, especially if you work in healthcare settings.

179.

Use a system in your appointment book that ensures confidentiality.

180.

Remember that if you both socialize and deal professionally with a community, you are better able to interpret in that community.

181.

If you have never experienced oppression, be sure to think of oppression when people are sharing their struggles as a minority person. I have seen majority interpreters miss the point in their interpretation because this experience was not part of their reality.

182.

Good transliteration is thought out.
If you are not thinking about what the speaker is saying, you are probably coding word-for-word, not transliterating.

183.

Review the use of classifiers in ASL.

184.

Deaf people are the experts
on their experience;
listen to their stories about
working with interpreters to
learn what you should strive
for as an interpreter.

185.

If a Deaf person is writing (or reading a handout) at a meeting while a hearing speaker is continuing to talk, be thoughtful and use your mind-mapping skills to recall the speaker's main points, so that when the Deaf person looks up again, you can fill her in.

186.

Attend a national interpreter convention if you haven't yet.

187.

Don't read magazines or pop novels at an assignment.

188.

Don't expect praise, but

do appreciate it

when it comes.

189.

What does it mean to be an *ally*?
It means acknowledging one's own
assumption of privilege and one's cultural
blind spots. It involves dealing honestly
with people, respecting a minority
person's ability to act, and negotiating
power so as to support the possibility
of an equal playing field.

190.

Be pleasant with consumers when not
interpreting; but when interpreting,
foremost, be on task.

191.

Be sure to have disability insurance.

192.

Always strive to adapt to

the language preference of

consumers, not have them

adapt to you.

193.

When you are signing, note if you are
using your voice (e.g., speaking in a
whisper) or making noise with your
hands. Either can be quite distracting
for hearing people.

194.

If you are a staff interpreter, make clear
distinctions between your tasks as a staff
member and your tasks as an interpreter.
Don't let these roles overlap.

195.

Learn all you can, but know your limits
and acknowledge them.

196.

When watching another

interpreter's work, look for what

you can learn. Don't miss these

golden opportunities.

197.

Professional ethics is not the same as personal ethics. Keep these separate, but make sure you have come to terms with your professional and personal ethical standards, so that they don't clash.

198.

If you are very nervous about an assignment, get some support from another interpreter and try to handle it the best you can. Consumers don't need to have to deal with our 'stuff'.

199.

If certain assignments cause you too much anxiety, don't accept them.

200.

Strive for—or maintain—

national certification.

201.

At the beginning of a meeting, try to get a sense of the group dynamics. For example, who is more likely to insist on having the floor, who is more *lassez-faire*, and who is more egalitarian in their approach? These factors need to come across in the interpretation.

202.

Be clear about billing and cancellation policies with those who hire you.

203.

Never go to an interpreting assignment without your appointment book.

204.

Don't forget that you will never truly know what it is like to be Deaf.

205.

Sometimes we define ourselves more by what we are against than what we are for. Don't get drawn into negativism; know what you are really for and let that be your guide.

206.

Make sure your invoices have all the pertinent data needed. For example, billing entities need to know how to contact you and often need your social security number to process your invoice.

207.

Don't give feedback unless it is requested and the person is open to feedback.

208.

Being considered trustworthy
is the key to a successful life as
an interpreter; it serves as a
necessary foundation for both
our interpreting work and our
ethical decisions.

209.

If you are transliterating for someone
who needs to read your lips,
mouth clearly and maintain
English word order. Don't slip into ASL
mouthing or ASL word order.

210.

In most settings, the Deaf participant(s)
should have the primary say in
where you position yourself.

211.

When interpreting in a dangerous
situation (such as a mental ward or a
jail), above all else, make sure you are
physically safe at all times.

212.

Some of the best wisdom on the

interpreting field is from Deaf

and hearing consumers.

Talk to them about how they see

interpreters, what they like, and

what they don't. Some of their

comments may surprise you.

213.

Be careful not to over-learn linguistic rules. Use them to help you structure your language production, but strive to understand what is most naturally used by native users.

214.

If someone is swearing or being offensive, be sure that comes across in the interpretation. At the same time, be sure that this is the person's intent. Not sure? Ask.

215.

Write a letter or an article for a newsletter.

216.

It is not enough to learn the

norms of a community;

try to understand the

underlying values. Most

cultural behaviors are

based on underlying values,

which are, by and large,

more generalizable.

217.

If there is a certain population or setting that is under-served in your area, consider specializing in that area to help fill the gap in services in the community.

218.

Study specialized terms from such fields as medicine and technology. Having even a sense of such terms can save the interpretation.

219.

Subscribe to Deaf community newsletters.

220.

If you make an error in an interpretation, own up to the fact it was the interpreter and not the speaker who needs to correct the message.

221.

Be aware that oppression generally happens because a person is unaware of how he is using privileges granted to him by society. Be on the lookout for how you may assume certain privileges at others' expense. Be aware, be honest, and be an ally.

222.

Do not use the term 'consumer' for just the Deaf person you work with; we work with Deaf *and* hearing consumers.

223.

Establish a set schedule for doing your billing and stick to it.

224.

Being focused and feeling confident lead to a successful interpretation; develop these in your work.

225.

If you are interpreting for someone who prefers ASL, maintain ASL word order and ASL non-manual modifiers. Don't slip into English mouthing or English word order (unless you determine that you need to convey something literally).

226.

Eat right and stay fit.

227.

Take adequate vacations.
Treat yourself, you deserve it.

228.

Remember that interpreters—

your colleagues—come from

all walks of life; expect and

respect this diversity.

229.

Remember if things aren't working in
an interpreting assignment,
stop the situation and re-negotiate.
You have that obligation.

230.

Always assume that whatever you say
about a consumer or another interpreter
will get back to that person.

231.

Every interpreter is not right for every
consumer. If a consumer prefers another
interpreter, realize that it is her choice
and it comes with the territory.

232.

Watch conversations among

native language users

(of ASL and English).

Attend to turn-taking and the

introduction of topics.

Strive to make the

conversations you interpret

follow natural discourse.

233.

The best way to learn, or increase your
fluency in, a second language is to be
among native users who forget you are
not a native user of the language.
You will see the language at work in a
natural environment.

234.

Support Deaf theater.

235.

Know your limits in specialized
settings. If you are in over your head,
you're not going to do much good
for the participants.

236.

Be sure to support other

interpreters, whether they are

newer or more experienced.

What we give, we receive.

237.

Many people avoid power, resent it, hold onto it, or feel compelled to follow anyone in a more powerful position. Deal with your power issues.

238.

Attend to the *goal* of the speaker; knowing that a person is trying to convince, motivate, or entertain an audience is the first step to understanding and conveying a clear equivalent message.

239.

Be aware of major holidays and events in other cultures.

240.

When a hearing interpreter and a Deaf interpreter team together, be sure that you work out beforehand how you will handle interpreting-related questions that come from either the Deaf consumer or the hearing consumer.

241.

Use judgment about where you speak
on the phone (especially a cell phone).
Be sure not to impose on people
who may not want to hear your phone
call, but also consider the possible
breach of confidentiality.

242.

Monitor the discourse structure of
the target language. Can the audience
follow what you are saying?

243.

Take on-going training appropriate for
your skill level. We all have important
things to learn and to work on.

244.

Be prepared to give a

thirty-second explanation

of your role and function

as an interpreter.

245.

Be aware of the differences between
learning in an academic setting
and learning in the community.
Each is beneficial, but each has its own
particular benefits. Engage in both.

246.

Study idioms in English so that you
understand them and have a
few possible interpretations ready
when you hear them.

247.

Have healthful snacks on hand.

248.

Treat all consumers with respect regardless of their position, socioeconomic status, ethnicity, hearing status, language preference, etc.

249.

When interpreting a long text into
English, try to use plural pronouns and
avoid the awkward phrase "he or she."
Five minutes of that would drive
anyone up the wall.

250.

Acknowledge the *languages* that we work
with (ASL and English); don't talk about
'modes of communication', which implies
something less than a language.

251.

Don't get so used to being a member
of 'third culture' that you forget what it
is like to be a 'hearing person'.

252.

Don't offer something that you can't deliver.

253.

Realize that consumers really do have an idea of what an interpreter does even if they have never worked with an interpreter before. Don't insult them by over-explaining the interpreter role.

254.

Sometimes interpreters must disagree with consumers, but remember *how* we communicate our position is as important as *why* we disagree.

255.

Keep your car in good repair.

256.

Remember that problems provide

opportunities to learn.

257.

Be aware that an interpreter needs to be easy to understand, so brush up on your enunciation (both spoken and signed).

258.

If you hold partial certification, only accept assignments that match your skill range and strive for full certification.

259.

Develop strategies for getting through the quick introductions that sometimes occur at the beginning of a meeting; the interpretation usually gets easier after the introductions.

260.

Note how you introduce yourself

to Deaf people and to hearing

people, as each group has

different cultural expectations

regarding introductions.

261.

Have pen and paper on hand to jot
down notes as needed.

262.

If you tend to not give yourself enough
process time, tell your team member
to remind you to wait before you
begin your interpretation; it can do
wonders for your interpreting.

263.

If you work as a staff interpreter, insist on
getting appropriate supervision and
support from an interpreter with more
training and experience than yourself.

264.

The tools of our trade are
language fluency, culture
awareness, managing the
interpreting process, and
quick decision-making. Make
sure that you have the latest
tools and that these tools are
honed and ready to use.

265.

If you interpret at the police station
or in the courtroom, be sure you are
qualified to do so and be sure to have
your interpretations videotaped.

266.

Develop some discourse 'openings'
that can help you get on
track right away.

267.

Deaf education is a hot topic.
Be aware of your own view, but respect
the educational diversity of members of
the Deaf community.

268.

Be aware of what interpreting

assignments you accept.

Be sure to accept a variety

of assignments, so that

the full range of the Deaf

community can be served.

269.

Do not make phone calls—or focus
on your pager—during an assignment
unless it is absolutely necessary,
and make sure people know that if you
are doing so, it is due to an urgent
matter. You are being paid to be present,
not to do other work.

270.

Avoid talking about important
issues with people who don't take
your views seriously.

271.

Warm up your voice as well as your arms
and hands before interpreting.

272.

Don't just copy or imitate
interpreting strategies used by
other interpreters. Figure out
what works for you given your
own personality and skills.

273.

Read relevant articles or books on
decision-making, cultural studies,
linguistics, ethics, business practices, and
interpersonal skills to increase your
ability to be a competent interpreter.

274.

Be aware of how you respond to
being tired and how you can
best counteract that response
when you are working.

275.

Fatigue is part mental and part
physical. Attend to both when you are
feeling drained.

276.

Feedback from Deaf consumers is a sign that they care and want you to do your best.

277.

If you interpret in the educational setting (K-12), be aware that you are a language model and that you will need to accommodate the developmental needs of the children.

278.

Always keep these two goals in mind when interpreting: *cohesiveness* and *clarity*.

279.

Remember that most mistakes can be forgiven—if we own them and allow ourselves to go on.

280.

Check with consumers to see

if the interpreting process is

working well for them.

You are showing you are

open to working with them

and they will find it easier

to work with you.

281.

Be aware that hearing consumers have
their own understanding of what it
means to be Deaf. That view may be
quite naive, informed, oppressive, or
indifferent. Expect differences and
develop strategies for working with
different consumers to provide an
effective interpretation.

282.

When deciding whether to sit or stand,
don't end up 'higher' than the
chairperson or speaker—unless
you need to stand to be seen by
the Deaf consumer(s).

283.

Be aware of how you work in a team and talk to your team interpreter about how you can best work together before you begin.

284.

If someone asks you to do something that you are uncomfortable with, don't just quote the Code of Ethics; rather, explain concisely and clearly why you cannot comply with the request. Remember:

1) you want to maintain a good working relationship with this person, and

2) you want this person to understand why you are turning down the request.

285.

An interpreter's tone of voice conveys a lot about mood and comfort level. Are you in control of your tone of voice when you interpret into English?

286.

Accept responsibility for

your decisions.

287.

If you are teaming with another interpreter, ride together if possible, and you can process the day together as well as enjoy your time in the car (or public transportation) catching up.

288.

If you get puzzled looks from consumers, be aware that the issue may not always be confusion over a particular concept. The confusion may stem from either an unclear section of discourse that was difficult to follow or a cultural difference that was not clear.

289.

Language learning never ends.

290.

Never forget the importance of

register; it reflects on the

speaker and how the speaker

is perceived.

291.

When you make an ethical decision,
stick to it even though it may be difficult,
and share with others your ethical
reasons for the decision.

292.

Remember when interpreting a job
interview or a job termination,
the *impressions* the participants are
making on each other (good or bad)
are very, very important.

293.

Don't stay up too late the night
before an assignment.

294.

Always accept criticism

graciously from consumers;

don't make excuses. Be thankful

for the advice and work to

remedy any issues they bring up.

295.

Remember that you work with
a lot of people, so you have lots of
'employers'. Strive to be a good
employee to all of them.

296.

If you struggle with the use of space,
establish a pattern that works for you.
For example, you may want to set
something up on the left first, then the
next thing on the right, then a third
thing in the center. You are more likely
to keep it all straight that way.

297.

Consider getting liability insurance.

298.

If you are not comfortable

with certain populations,

be true to your feelings and

don't accept assignments with

these populations.

299.

When interpreting in a counseling
session, expect that you may experience
transference from the client. Maintain
your boundaries, and realize you may
become part of this person's therapy.

300.

Be sure you keep up the strength
in your hands and wrists if you do a
lot of Deaf-Blind interpreting.

301.

Codependence has no place in an
interpreter's life. Get good counseling
before you put yourself in the middle
of other people's lives.

302.

Read the latest book on
interpreting. It can broaden
your understanding and
motivate you to try something
new in your work.

303.

Interpreters must determine people's worldview to interpret accurately; however, be sure not to pigeon-hole people or to jump to conclusions too quickly. There is much diversity within a cultural group; don't over-generalize.

304.

If you are aware of the lack of skills of a certain segment of the interpreting field, work with that group to improve. Finger-pointing doesn't get us anywhere, and if you don't act, you are part of the problem.

305.

Attitude is ninety percent of the job.

306.

When working as part of an interpreting team, remember foremost that the team has a common goal and shares the responsibility for the interpreting work.

307.

Sometimes interpreters try to 'get every
word in', but don't let 'all the words'
get in the way. Usually, fewer
well-chosen words are clearer to those
depending on the interpretation.

308.

Some things just don't translate;
find the best equivalent you can,
but if you can't find an equivalent,
be clear in your interpretation that you
can't do justice to the message.

309.

Call for directions or get directions on the
Internet; it can save a lot of headaches.

310.

If you interpret for children, keep up to date about the latest cartoons, toys, music, and technology for children; these topics are going to come up.

311.

Our goal is to equalize the power in
terms of communication, but we will
see oppression at work at times.
Realize that providing the means for
people to communicate is a step away
from oppression.

312.

Transliterate only when the
consumer asks you directly to do so
or when the consumer obviously
prefers transliteration.

313.

Be aware of your process time and vary
it as needed—depending on the text.

314.

Remember that interpreting

is both an art *and* a science;

don't attend to one of these at

the expense of the other.

315.

Don't ignore hearing consumers.
Occasionally make eye contact with
them, but, at the same time,
be careful not to allow them to
become too aligned with you.

316.

Have light reading with you in
case you're stuck waiting before an
assignment begins.

317.

If you interpret in a religious setting,
work with your church, synagogue,
or temple to provide the best
interpreting services possible.

318.

Be sure to give back to the Deaf community. Volunteer.

319.

When interpreting a play into ASL or English, be sure to put in the time to do justice to this artistic work.

320.

Be aware that we need to be mentally healthy because we are smack-dab in the middle of other people's lives.

321.

If you interpret in an educational setting (K-12), support Deaf students' contact with the Deaf community, and maintain your own contact with the Deaf community as well.

322.

Work as part of an interpreting

team whenever possible;

two heads are better than one.

323.

If you are a staff interpreter, scheduling is crucial. Be sure to work as a team when necessary (due to length of time or dense content) and hire outside interpreters as needed.

324.

When getting ready to interpret a telephone call, don't make a big deal about *who* dials; do whatever is most convenient.

325.

When discarding paper documents, shred those which contain confidential information.

326.

Remember that in some situations it may be best to negotiate for consecutive interpretation instead of doing simultaneous interpretation.

327.

If you are on call for an emergency,
be prepared to drop what you are doing;
you have an obligation to go.

328.

Don't over-focus on the Source Language
or the Target Language in your
interpreting work; it is usually more
beneficial to focus on how you are
managing the interpreting process.

329.

If there is a conflict between
yourself and a consumer or another
interpreter, be sure to look at your own
behavior before addressing
the issue with the other person.

330.

Be honest about your

mistakes, but learn from

your mistakes.

331.

Don't expect a team interpreter to just correct errors. A team interpreter can confirm that you are on the right track, can hand you a glass of water, and can offer you possible language choices. This person provides you an opportunity to get the support you need.

332.

Don't yawn. It doesn't look professional and yawns are terribly contagious.

333.

The Golden Rule applies to interpreters, too. Treat others as you want to be treated.

334.

Don't assume you know enough

about your native language.

There's always more to learn.

335.

If you are waiting only two or three
seconds before you begin your
interpretation, you are not doing justice
to the interpretation. Be sure you have a
good sense of what someone is saying
before you begin the interpretation.

336.

Don't eat onions or garlic for lunch.

337.

If you use an ASL dictionary,
be sure to double check with
native signers about how to sign the
concepts you look up.

338.

Don't forget either the

hearing or Deaf consumer's

feelings and perspective.

339.

Just as you may judge others by what they do and not just by what they say, remember others may be judging you by what you do, not just what you say.

340.

Establish a working rapport with consumers that is situationally and culturally appropriate. Be aware that Deaf rapport and hearing rapport differ.

341.

Speak up when a person wants to jump in, especially when this is a Deaf person or other minority person.

342.

We are paid for what we

know and what we *do*;

both need constant nurturing.

343.

When interpreting a play, be sure that
the story line and character development
are clear in the interpretation.

344.

Before interpreting a telephone call, get
the name of the person being called and
the general purpose of the call.

345.

Being a member of a disenfranchised
group may help you identify with another
group that is also disenfranchised.
At the same time, be sure that it doesn't
cloud your judgment.

346.

Matching our actions to our

values gives us *integrity*, which

is at the heart of ethics.

347.

Develop strategies for wording a participant's desire to jump into a conversation. "I have something to say" is overused by interpreters and less effective than other strategies, such as simply saying the name of the person who is running the meeting.

348.

Practice relaxation and focus techniques before high-pressure interpreting work.

349.

Avoid the phrase, 'My consumer'; it implies possession.

350.

Try not to dictate language choice. If a hearing person wishes to sign during a meeting, or if a Deaf person prefers transliteration, we are there to meet their needs.

351.

If a problem arises, be sure to be aware of the root of the problem. Is it an ethical issue? A cultural issue? A power issue?

352.

Let people know that there will be a slight pause between the time a question is asked and an answer is rendered due to the process time you need as an interpreter. If people know what to expect, they are more willing to be flexible and to work with you.

353.

Support Deaf-run religious institutions.

354.

Talk to more experienced interpreters about the interpreting process, making ethical decisions, and their suggestions for training.

355.

Be aware of the fiscal year of the entities whom you bill, and always send your invoices within the same fiscal year that you provide the interpreting services.

356.

We are trained to hang up our emotions before beginning an assignment.
If you practice that, don't lose track of your emotions.

357.

Remember your *face* when you sign.
Are you using ASL grammatical markers?
Are you showing affect?

358.

Be aware that ethical decisions
involving the young and
the old may play out differently,
due to differences in
experience, expectations,
and vulnerability.

359.

Make a list of 'literalisms' that are
overused by interpreters that aren't
used by native users of the language,
and avoid these.

360.

If you're struggling with understanding
something about your interpreting,
try using a metaphor, analogy, model, or
theory when discussing it with someone
else; it may prove enlightening.

361.

Be aware of when to topicalize in ASL.
Look at the key moments in discourse
when topicalization is used, and use
topicalization strategically.

362.

If a consumer is saying, "Tell him" or "Tell her," this tells you more about how this person perceives the interpreting role than it does this person's attitude. Deal with this fairly.

363.

Be sure that you don't convey a
speaker's *content* (information) at the
expense of the speaker's *goal* (intent).

364.

Remember that you are an expert on
interpretation, but you are not an expert
on being Deaf. If you are asked questions
about Deaf people, know your limits—
and refer these questions to Deaf people.

365.

When setting goals for yourself,
think about what you *can* do, and
don't just focus on what you *can't*.